LET'S GO
FISHING
FOR SHELLFISH

George Travis

The Rourke Corporation, Inc.
Vero Beach, Florida 32964

PHOTO CREDITS:
© Richard K. Davis/North Carolina Department of Marine Fisheries: cover,
page 13; © Jeff Greenberg/International Stock: page 4; © Michael
Ventura/International Stock: page 12; © International Stock: page 15;
© United States Coast Guard/District page 13: page 16; © East Coast
Studios: pages 7, 10; © Corel: pages 6, 9, 18, 19

FISH ILLUSTRATIONS: © Duane Raver

PROJECT EDITOR: Duane Raver
Duane Raver received a degree in Zoology with a major in fishery
management from Iowa State University. Employed by the North Carolina
Wildlife Resources Commission as a fishery biologist in 1950, he
transferred to the Education Division in 1960. He wrote and illustrated for
the magazine *Wildlife in North Carolina*. Mr. Raver retired as the editor in
1979 and is a freelance writer and illustrator.

EDITORIAL SERVICES: Penworthy Learning Systems

Library of Congress Cataloging-in-Publication Data

Travis, George. 1961-
    Let's go fishing for shellfish / by George Travis.
        p. cm. — (Let's go fishing)
    Includes index
    ISBN 0-86593-466-5
    1. Shellfish gathering—Juvenile literature. I. Title.
II. Series: Travis, George, 1961 Let's go fishing.
SH400.4.T735 1998
799.2'54—dc21   97–49078
                                                                      CIP
                                                                      AC

Printed in the USA

TABLE OF CONTENTS

WHAT ARE SHELLFISH?

Shellfish are animals that have hard shells and live mostly in water. There are two main groups of shellfish, **crustaceans** (kruh STAY shunz) and **mollusks** (MAHL usks).

Crustaceans have tough outer shells with several pairs of legs. Lobsters, crabs, and shrimp are crustaceans.

Mollusks have soft, fleshy bodies that are covered with hard shells. Clams, oysters, and mussels are mollusks.

Shellfish, like most other fish, are caught to be eaten and enjoyed. Shrimp and crabs are sometimes used as bait.

Most crustaceans and mollusks are caught with traps or nets, not with lines and hooks.

This man pulls several king crabs from a crab pot.

SHRIMP

Many kinds of shrimp live in our waters. You can find shrimp in many saltwater areas. They are gray-green when alive. When cooked in hot water, they turn pink.

There are certain seasons when you can go shrimping. Shrimp can be found in the water near shelters—rock piles, weeds, and wooden piers.

Many people enjoy eating shrimp.

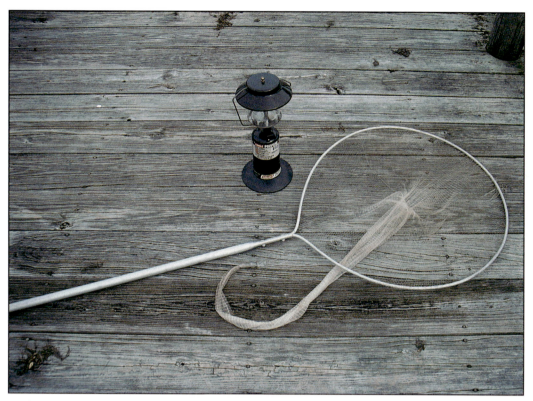

A hand net and lantern can be used to catch shrimp.

A hand net is one way to catch these little shellfish. Shrimp are most active on cloudy days. You can even go shrimping at night. Use a light to see their eyes before you scoop them up in a net.

Shrimp are rich in vitamins, minerals, and protein. Besides being low in fat, they taste good.

LOBSTERS

Lobsters are large crustaceans with ten legs and a long body and broad tail. The American lobster is the best-known member of the lobster family. They live in the cold North Atlantic Ocean. Some are found as far south as North Carolina.

Their front legs form large claws. Their claws help to fight off **predators** (PRED uh turz). At the same time, the claws help the lobster to catch its food.

The spiny lobster lives along the southeast coast of the U.S. It has stiff, sharp antennas instead of claws.

Lobster traps, or pots, are placed underwater on the sandy bottom. They can be checked on days later. It is important to flag the traps to make them easy to find.

When put in the water, these pots may catch a nice lobster.

CRABS

Many kinds of crabs live in our oceans. The crabs that people most like to eat are blue crabs, snow crabs, and king crabs.

Some people fish for blue crabs by dipping lines baited with chunks of meat. Traps, or pots, are used to catch crabs, too. The pots are made of **twine** (TWYN) or wire. People take them out to sea by boat and leave them for several days. Fresh fish is placed inside the traps to attract the crabs.

Crabs can usually get out of a trap if they want to, but often they choose to stay in it. They think they have found a good place to live!

Crabs have to be handled carefully—their claws can give you a nasty pinch!

MOLLUSKS

Cockles, mussels, clams, and oysters have two shells with a hinge that opens and closes. Their shells protect their soft bodies from predators. Mollusks, like conch and winkles, have just one shell to hide in.

Clams filter water through their bodies to eat and breathe.

This boat comes into dock with a full load of shellfish.

Mussels and winkles are usually the easiest shellfish to find. They like to cling to weeds and rocks. Clams and cockles bury themselves in the sand, so you need a small rake to find them. Small hollow places in the sand are good spots to dig for them.

Oysters are becoming so rare that you are not likely to find many. Most oysters for sale are grown on oyster farms.

POISONED SHELLFISH

People have become sick from eating bad shellfish. Sometimes these shellfish live in **polluted** (puh LOOT ed) water.

Mollusks like oysters, mussels, and clams are harmed by polluted water the most because they must filter water through their bodies to eat and breathe. If the water is polluted, poisons end up in the bodies of shellfish.

Raw oysters are a **delicacy** (DEL eh kuh see) enjoyed by many people. Some restaurants will not serve raw seafood because of the danger of food poisoning.

Pollution in the water is not good for shellfish—or for you!

RULES & REGULATIONS

Most governments set rules for catching shellfish. These rules keep fishermen and trappers from overfishing certain areas or fishing in polluted waters.

State government agencies, like the California Department of Fish and Game, make sure the rules are obeyed by the local fishing industry. The state agency is also the one that requires you to buy a fishing license.

Also, federal regulations and rules apply to certain waters of all states in the U.S. The federal agencies that help manage these waters are the National Marine Fisheries Service and the U.S. Fish and Wildlife Service.

U.S. Coast Guard patrols offshore fishing grounds.

PREPARED FOR MARKET

One of the tastiest foods you can buy in a restaurant or grocery store is shellfish. Stores sell it frozen or fresh. Restaurants sell it grilled, fried, or cooked any other way you like.

After buying lobster from the market, it can be cooked on a grill.

This market has many kinds of shellfish.

Stores that sell shellfish usually buy it from a seafood **distributor** (di STRIB yuh tur). Before distributors can sell seafood, they must buy it from **commercial** (kuh MER shul) fishermen, who catch it.

Several people help get the seafood from the sea to the store before you can buy it.

SHELLFISH FARMING

Shellfish farming is a form of **aquaculture** (AK wuh KUL chur), the growing of sea animals or plants for food.

Shellfish are farmed in different ways; but all are farmed or grown in a controlled, or closed-in, area.

Each year Americans eat so many shellfish that the oceans and rivers are becoming **depleted** (di PLEET ed) of this wonderful food source. The best way to prevent this is to raise shellfish on farms instead of taking them from the ocean.

fish: American lobster *(Homarus americanus)*
average weight: less than 1 lb.
(.45 kilograms), may reach
45 lbs. (10.3 kilograms)
location: eastern coast of
North America from
Cape Hatteras to
southern Labrador

---

fish: American oyster *(Crassostrea virginica)*
average weight: less than 1 lb. (.45 kilograms)
location: Brazil
northward through the
Carribean and Gulf of
Mexico to the Saint
Lawrence River

---

fish: blue crab *(Callinecteus sapidus)*
average weight: less than 1 lb.
(.45 kilograms)
location: mostly in Chesapeake
Bay area, south Atlantic and
Gulf states

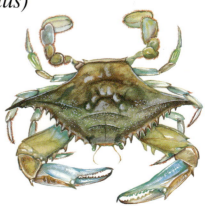

fish: common shrimp (*Penaeus setiferus*)
average weight: 2 to 3 ozs.
(567 to 850 grams)
location: Atlantic coast
from Virginia to Texas and
Brazil

---

fish: eastern surf clam (*Spisula solidissima*)
average weight: less than 1 lb.
(.45 kilograms)
location: Maine to
South Carolina

---

fish: snow crab (*Chionoectes opilio*)
average weight: about 1 lb.
(.45 kilograms)
location: North Atlantic,
North Pacific from Alaska
to Northern California

GLOSSARY

aquaculture (AK wuh KUL chur) — the process of farming shellfish in enclosed areas, where they are fed to grow faster than in their natural environment

commercial (kuh MER shul) — buying and selling goods, what people do to make money

crustaceans (kruh STAY shunz) — group of shellfish that have tough outer shells and several pairs of legs

delicacy (DEL eh kuh see) — an especially fine quality food; a special food that people love to eat

depleted (di PLEET ed) — less, reduced numbers of, emptied out

distributor (di STRIB yuh tur) — a person who sells goods, such as fish, to stores in large numbers

mollusks (MAHL usks) — group of shellfish that have soft, fleshy bodies and one or two hard outer shells

predator (PRED uh tur) — an animal that eats other animals

polluted (puh LOOT ed) — made dirty, poisoned

twine (TWYN) — a strong cord made of two or more strands twisted together

INDEX

FURTHER READING:

Find out more about fishing with these helpful books and information sites:
The Dorling Kindersley Encyclopedia of Fishing. The Complete Guide to the Fish, Tackle, & Techniquies of Fresh & Saltwater Angling. Dorling Kindersley, Inc., 1994
Price, Steven D. *The Ultimate Fishing Guide.* HarperCollins, 1996
Waszczuk, Henry and Labignan, Halto. *Freshwater Fishing. 1000 Tips from the Pros.* Key Porter Books, 1993
Fishernet online at www.thefishernet.com
National Marine Fisheries Service online at www.nmfs.gov
World of Fishing online at www.fishingworld.com